ABOUT ANT & DEC

Ant & Dec first appeared on TV screens over 30 years ago, starring in a children's show called *Byker Grove*. Since then, they've hosted some of the UK's best loved shows, including *Saturday Night Takeaway*, *Britain's Got Talent* and *I'm a Celebrity . . . Get Me Out of Here*. They have won over 40 National Television Awards and 13 BAFTAs, and have even topped the UK charts in 2013, with 'Let's Get Ready to Rhumble', a re-release of the most famous hit from their pop career.

They are NSPCC Ambassadors for Childhood, and all their proceeds from sales of *Propa Happy* will go to support the NSPCC.

Ant & Dec were both born and raised in Newcastle.

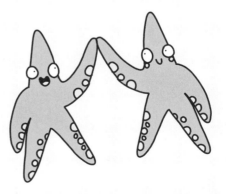

To all the children helped by the NSPCC.

Propa Happy was created in consultation with a child psychology expert and with guidance from the NSPCC.

NSPCC: Registered charity England and Wales 216401, Scotland SC037717 and Jersey 384.

First published in Great Britain 2022 by Red Shed, part of Farshore
An imprint of HarperCollins*Publishers*
1 London Bridge Street, London SE1 9GF
www.farshore.co.uk

HarperCollins*Publishers*
1st Floor, Watermarque Building,
Ringsend Road, Dublin 4, Ireland

Text copyright © Ant McPartlin and Declan Donnelly 2022
Ant McPartlin and Declan Donnelly have asserted their moral rights.
Illustrations copyright © HarperCollins*Publishers* 2022
Illustrations by Katie Abey.
Cover photograph (faces) © Robert Wilson 2022
Cover photograph (clothing) © Getty 2022
Consultancy by Dr Miquela Walsh, DEdPsych,
MsC (Dist), BSc (Hons), HCPC accredited.

LEGO® is a trademark of the LEGO Group of companies
which does not sponsor, authorise or endorse this book.

ISBN 978 0 00852 434 0
Printed in Italy
001

ANT & DEC

PROPA Happy

WITH ANDY MILLIGAN

ILLUSTRATED BY KATIE ABEY

RED SHED

CONTENTS

PROPA HAPPY PEOPLE!

We asked you, the readers, to tell us about your friends, your favourite things and what makes you happy. Look out for the answers in these special clouds . . .

Dancing, singing and going to the zoo make me happy!

Ava, age 9

HELLO, READERS!

Ant: I'm Ant and he's Dec. Welcome to our book!

Dec: You might have seen us on something called 'the telly', where we love to have a laugh and try to make other people feel good.

Ant: And feeling good is what this book is all about. It's full of our favourite games, jokes, activities ... and ways to help you find **YOUR** happy.

Dec: And one of the ways to do that is to remember that you're completely unique. No two people are the same – not even me and Ant.

Ant: This book is also about those moments when you don't feel like smiling. We all have them and it's important to recognise that. This book will help you check in and say what's on your mind.

Dec: What's on **YOUR** mind, Ant?

Ant: I want to read this book!

Dec: Me too! So what are we waiting for?
Let's get Propa Happy!

BE PROUD

to let others see how

AMAZING

you are!

THE PROUD
PANTHER

CHAPTER 1

ALL ABOUT YOU

Happiness comes from inside us – and it means different things to all of us. Maybe your friends all love football, but you prefer drama. Perhaps you love to talk and your siblings are quieter. **BE YOUR OWN PERSON!** Know what you love – and celebrate what makes you different. This chapter is all about YOU and what makes you unique.

WHO ARE YOU?
Quiz

Ant: We're starting with a big question –
who are you?

Dec: I'm Dec. I'm your best friend!

Ant: No, no! I mean, what is unique about the person
reading this book! It might be your likes and
dislikes, skills, strengths or dreams for the future.

Dec: Why not give this quiz a shot, to see what type of
person you might be ...

1. How many siblings do you have?
 a) None.
 b) One.
 c) Two or more.
 d) I have siblings, but I think they're
   aliens in disguise.

2. Where do you live?
 a) In a city or town.
 b) In the countryside.
 c) With an old woman in a shoe.
 d) In a giant palace made of chocolate (I wish!).

3. **What's your favourite lesson at school?**
a) Maths or Science.
b) History, Geography or English.
c) Art or PE.
d) The bit where I get to go home!

4. **What is your favourite hobby?**
a) Playing sports.
b) Baking cakes.
c) Drawing.
d) Reading books written by cool TV double acts.

5. **Which word best describes you?**
a) Clever.
b) Creative.
c) Fun.
d) Good at questionnaires. Oops, that's three words.

6. **How are you feeling right now?**
a) Grumpy.
b) Happy.
c) Excited.
d) Too excited to answer this question.

7. **Pick a dream job:**
a) Fastest runner in the whole wide world.
b) Chef.
c) Can I have a bit of time to think about this one?
d) Intergalactic time traveller.

TURN OVER TO FIND OUT WHO YOU ARE!

WHO ARE YOU?
Quiz answers

IF YOU ANSWERED . . .

Mostly As: Congratulations!
You are an amazing, unique person!

Mostly Bs: Congratulations!
You are an amazing, unique person!

Mostly Cs: Congratulations!
You are an amazing, unique person!

Mostly Ds: Congratulations!
You are an amazing, unique person!

Ant: OK, you may have spotted something — it doesn't matter which answers you chose, because whatever you like or dislike, are good at or find challenging, **YOU ARE AN AMAZING, UNIQUE PERSON**!

Why not share this quiz with a friend or family member?

WHAT MAKES YOU YOU?

IT'S YOUR QUALITIES
Are you courageous?
Caring? Sporty? Silly?

IT'S YOUR EXPERIENCES
Where have you
lived or visited?
What have you learned?

IT'S WHAT YOU LIKE
What's your favourite food?
Your favourite song?

IT'S YOUR GOALS
What do you want to
achieve this week?
Or this year?

SINGING
SUPERSTAR

GLOBETROTTER

THE TALENTED TOAD

FOOTBALL
FAN

FASHION-
FORWARD

Ant: There's no one single thing that makes you who you are today. And it's the same for us two. What are some of the things that make you *you*, Dec?

Dec: Well, I love a good natter! And I love fascinating facts, like ... wombats have square poo!

Ant: **GOOD POO FACT!** Me, I love reading, cooking, muddy dog walks ...

Dec: It's a whole COLLAGE of things!

Ant: Right, it's time to go to Collage College ...

13

ALL ABOUT ME
Collage

You'll need:
- Paper
- Coloured pens
- Glue
- Pictures and objects that represent you

STEP 1:

Find a piece of paper.
The bigger, the better!

STEP 2:

Write your name on the paper.
This collage is all about **YOU**.

STEP 3:

Now collect things that represent **YOU**. They could
be drawings or pictures cut out from magazines
or photos of your friends and family. It could even
be real 3D objects, like ticket stubs, cards, feathers
or beads.

IF THEY'RE SOMEONE ELSE'S
PHOTOS OR MAGAZINES,
DON'T FORGET TO CHECK
THAT IT'S OK TO USE THEM.

Arrange all the pieces of 'you', and ask an adult to help you glue them to the paper. **TA-DA!** You could also write down things that make you happy on the collage.

HERE ARE **SOME** EXAMPLES . . .

Ant: I love cooking.

Dec: And I love eating!

Ant: That's what makes us such a great team!

Ant & Dec: We love Newcastle United, golf and watching TV.

Ant: I love movie night.

Ant: No one else's collage will look like yours — because no one else is just like you!

Dec: Not feeling crafty? Try talking about or acting out the things that would make up your collage.

HAPPINESS IS . . .

My baby brother!

Eyad, age 7

Waking up and seeing the sunshine because it makes me be in a positive mood.

Kyran, age 9

When something good happens like winning a football match.

Will, age 11

Seeing my friends and going to the funfair.

Sophia, age 10

Dancing, music and painting. And being weird!

Flo, age 9

Making my grandma laugh, playing with Dashie, my hamster, and listening to the *Hamilton* soundtrack.

Elliot, age 10

My friends! We help each other if we get stuck.

Elijah, age 6

When there is something fun to do or when I reach a goal.

Ibrahim, age 9

THE POWER OF POSITIVITY

Ant: How is your day going? Are you having fun? Maybe something important hasn't gone to plan? Whatever challenging things are going on, you'll always find something that makes you feel good if you look closely enough.

Dec: Looking for stuff that makes you feel good is called positivity.

Ant: Positivity is a kind of superpower that will help you deal with all sorts of challenges.

Challenges might be anything from making a mistake to a life-changing event. Whatever the challenge, take a moment to try to notice those things that give you a boost when you need it most.

SO, WHAT POWERS YOUR POSITIVITY? TIME TO FIND OUT . . .

ACTIVATE YOUR POWER OF POSITIVITY

Time to tap into your positivity superpower in just one minute! Can you think of **THREE** things that made you feel good today?

HERE ARE SOME EXAMPLES . . .

I TOLD A JOKE THAT MADE PEOPLE LAUGH.

THE SUN CAME OUT.

I READ MY FAVOURITE BOOK BY A REALLY COOL TV DOUBLE ACT.

ME AND MY FRIENDS MADE UP SOME NEW GAMES.

Ant: So there you go, be positive whenever you can!

Dec: Are you sure?

Ant: I'm positive!

Dec: Nice!

THE PANGOLIN OF POSITIVITY

BE MORE YOU-NICORN
A story about being yourself

Corey the Unicorn lived in Rainbow Meadow. He had lots of friends – but he felt different. He didn't much like rainbows – all those colours made his eyes hurt. He liked reading, playing video games and ballet dancing. Especially ballet dancing.

Corey went to the chief unicorn. "I am the **WORST UNICORN IN THE WORLD**," he said. "I wish I liked Normal Unicorn Things."

To his surprise, the chief unicorn smiled. "Being different is what makes you special, Corey! Now look closer . . ."

So Corey looked. He saw lots of unicorns skipping over rainbows. He ALSO saw unicorns playing badminton, baking cookies . . . and doing all kinds of things. There was no such thing as a Normal Unicorn. Every unicorn was different! **Every unicorn was UNI-QUE!**

YOUR TURN

Don't worry about how others see you.
It doesn't matter what other people think about how you look or what you wear. What matters is being true to yourself.

Do the hobbies you love.
Don't worry if it's not what your friends are into. When they see how much fun you're having, they'll probably want to try your hobbies too!

Be confident about who you are.
Instead of comparing yourself to others, try to take time to appreciate yourself. After all, there is only one **YOU**!

Ant: Remember, no two people are the same. The Universe would be such a boring place if we all thought in the same way.

Dec: Remember, no two people are the same. The Universe would be such a boring place if we all thought in the same way.

Ant: I've got a funny feeling I've heard that somewhere before...

MEET FUTURE YOU

Ant: There's someone we'd like you to meet...

Dec: Future You!

Ant: Future You may have won an Olympic medal, starred in a movie, invented a new type of breakdancing vegetable or gone all day without farting.

Dec: That's quite an achievement!

Ant: But what Future You really wants is to look back at what their life – **YOUR life** – was like. If only there was some way of capturing your life now...

Dec: Hang on, there is a way... make a video time capsule – something you can revisit in a year, ten years... or even 100 years!

CELEBRATE ALL THE THINGS THAT ARE IMPORTANT TO YOU RIGHT NOW!

THE TIME-TRAVELLING TORTOISE

HOW TO MAKE
a video time capsule

STEP 1:

Use your phone or video camera (or borrow one from a trusted adult) to record moments such as:

YOUR LIFE
What is important to you right now? What are you proud of?

THE NEWS
What is going on in the world? Don't forget to say what year it is!

YOUR FRIENDS AND FAMILY
What have they been up to?

YOUR HOUSE
Take a tour!

STEP 2:

Add a message for Future You – what do you wish for your future self?

DEC'S TOP TIP: If you're not a film fan, make a physical time capsule instead. Collect photos or objects, and write down memories.

Remember: If you're filming someone else, ask their permission first. And never post anything online without checking with a trusted adult.

FILM OF YOUR LIFE

Ant: Right, get ready to shout **'ACTION'** through a megaphone, because we're all going to Hollywood!

Dec: All of us? Us AND all the people reading this book?

Ant: No, Dec, I meant—

Dec: We're going to need a massive plane – and where are we going to stay when we get there?

Ant: DECLAN! WE ARE NOT ACTUALLY GOING TO ACTUAL HOLLYWOOD! This activity is about using your imagination. Imagine there was going to be a movie made all about you and your life. What kind of movie would it be: serious or funny? Action or fantasy? What important parts of your life would be in it? What would you change or keep the same? Remember, what's in a film doesn't have to be realistic!

Dec: Ohhh, that sounds like fun! And we are available for acting work – can we audition?

MAKE a movie poster

Once you've got some ideas for your movie, why not make a poster for it?

STEP 1:

Think of a film title – something that will give the audience a flavour of what the film is about.

Ant: *The Adventures of the Amazingly Awesome Ant.* Everyone would go and see that; it'll be a big hit!

Dec: Mine's going to be *Frozen 3*.

Ant: You can't just use the title of a film that's already successful.

Dec: Watch me.

STEP 2:

Think of a tagline – this might be a phrase that you love to say!

Ant: My tagline would be: 'He's Definitely the Best Out of Ant & Dec.' Dec, what would yours be?

Dec: How about: 'It Might Not Have Anyone From *Frozen 1* or *2* in it.'

STEP 3:

Design the poster. You could use photos of yourself – or you could draw or paint something new!

THE POWER OF GRATITUDE

Think about all those times you have food on your plate, a warm bed, and friends and family to support you. By stopping to appreciate all the things you have, you're using the power of gratitude.

Ant: Let's both list things we're grateful for, Dec.

Dec: Great idea! I'll start. I'm grateful for my family and a job I love. And I'm also grateful for Ant—

Ant: Aw, thanks!

Dec: Let me finish. I'm very grateful for Anti-Freeze when my car windscreen freezes up.

Ant: Charming! My turn. I'm grateful for my family. I'm grateful that I get to make people laugh on TV. And I'm grateful for that little guy I take for walks and who wees in my garden.

Dec: Your dog?

Ant: No, I meant you!

Dec: I wish you'd let me use the toilet in your house.

ACTIVATE YOUR POWER OF GRATITUDE

Time to channel your power of gratitude! Can you think of **THREE** things you are grateful for?

HERE ARE SOME EXAMPLES . . .

MY BEST FRIEND WHO LAUGHS AT ALL MY JOKES.

MY HAMSTER.

MY FAVOURITE SANDWICH AT LUNCHTIME.

RIDING MY SCOOTER.

I ALSO LOVE YOUR JOKES!

And don't stop there:

IF SOMEONE DOES SOMETHING YOU'RE GRATEFUL FOR, GIVE THEM A BIG THANK YOU!

WE CHALLENGE YOU

Decorate your space

Whether you share a bedroom or have it to yourself, it's important to have a space that's special to you – however small. This is a place that feels safe and relaxing. It's somewhere special you can **think, dream** and **be yourself**.

FINDING YOUR SPACE

Your space could be your bedroom, if you're lucky enough to have one of your own. It could also be a corner of a room – or even your bed. If you're not sure where your own personal space is, talk to a grown-up you trust. Ask them to help you **make a space just for YOU**.

Ant: First things first, we need to change the title to: Ant & Dec-orate Your Space.

Dec: Yes! Love it!

FIND YOUR
SPACE, MAN!

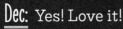

ANT & DEC-ORATE YOUR SPACE

Use colour

If you're lucky enough to have your own room, ask your parent or guardian if you can paint the walls in your favourite colour. If not, paint a picture or create a collage in that colour.

Make it personal

You can find lots of things at charity shops to decorate your room, or ask an adult to help you upcycle old furniture!

ANT'S TOP TIP: Add photos of your friends, family or your favourite celebrities. You could pin these to a cork board or hang up photo frames.

Look down, look up

Don't forget about the spaces below your feet and above your head. You could make a cosy pile of cushions on the floor, hang fairy lights or add glow-in-the-dark stars.

Dream space

Maybe finding somewhere to call your own is difficult right now. Ask yourself, if you could create a space of your own, what would it be like? Draw or describe somewhere that makes you feel safe and happy. Add as much detail as you can!

HOW TO MAKE
a proud cloud

Ant: Every day, we learn. Every day, we grow. We've all come so far since the day we were born. We should be **PROUD** of ourselves!

Dec: Is that a proud cloud I see before me?

WHY NOT MAKE A PROUD CLOUD TO CELEBRATE YOUR ACHIEVEMENTS?

You'll need:
- Paper or card
- Glue
- Scissors
- Your imagination

STEP 1:

Ask an adult to help you cut a piece of paper or card into mini clouds.

STEP 2:

Make a list of things you're proud of. Write them all down on mini clouds and, with the help of your adult, glue them to a second piece of paper or card.

HERE ARE A FEW IDEAS
TO GET YOU STARTED . . .

I'M PROUD THAT I DID MY CHORES WITHOUT BEING REMINDED.

I'M PROUD THAT I WORKED REALLY HARD ON MY SCHOOL PROJECT.

I'M PROUD THAT I NEVER GIVE UP, EVEN WHEN I CAN'T DO SOMETHING STRAIGHT AWAY.

DEC'S TOP TIP: Not feeling like writing today? You could draw a picture, make up a poem or tell someone about the things you are proud of.

Psst . . . What pants do clouds wear?

THUNDERWEAR!

31

I BELONG HERE

Happiness comes from within – but feeling connected to others – your family, friends and community – is an important part of who we all are.

Ant: Who do you feel connected to, Dec?

Dec: My family, my friends – and my home city, Newcastle. It's always been a big part of my identity. I love the people there, who are always so friendly, and of course, the football team.

Ant: I'm also from Newcastle and I love the place and how full of history it is. You've got Roman forts, the Quayside, Hadrian's Wall – I love history! Then there's that amazing feeling when you're on the train home and you see the Tyne Bridge. It always sends a shiver down my spine.

Dec: I get the same shiver when I drive home and see the Angel of the North.

Ant: You drive home? You always say you're going on the train so you can't give me a lift . . .

Dec: Let's move on, shall we?

YOUR TURN

Who are your family and friends? Take a moment to think about the important people in your life who support you and care about you.

Where do you live? What do you like about it and is there anything about it you would change? Have you lived in other places? What are your memories?

THE BADGERS OF BELONGING

What other communities are you part of? A community is any group of people you feel connected to – maybe your class, school or a club you belong to. How do you feel when you spend time with them?

What if I don't feel connected? Maybe you feel alone and that you don't belong? We all feel this way from time to time. Try talking to someone you trust, who may be able to help you figure out why and what you can do.

Remember: Belonging isn't the same as 'fitting in' – it's about being accepted just as you are, and feeling connected.

TRUE FRIENDS

are the ones

WHO LOVE US

just the way we are!

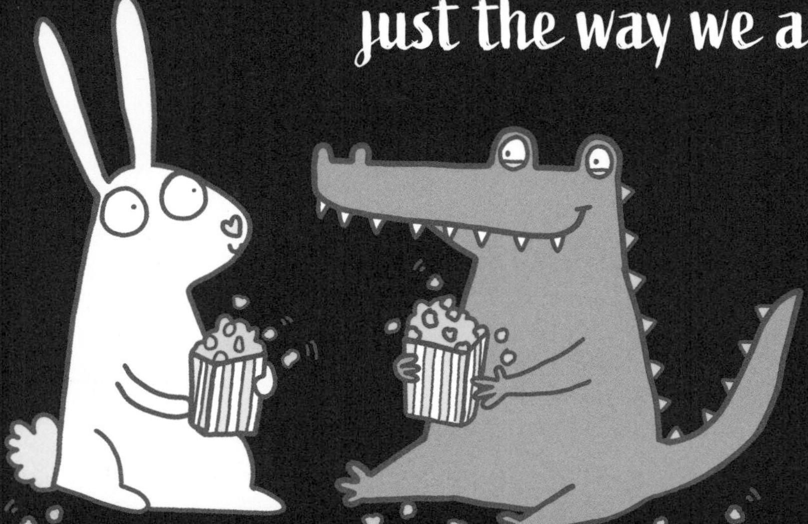

CHAPTER 2

FRIENDS MATTER

Our friends are the people who get us. The ones who make us laugh and who are there for us when we're having a bad day. You might have one friend or twenty – it doesn't matter. What counts is that **OUR FRIENDS MAKE US FEEL GOOD**. This chapter is all about getting to know our friends better, making new friends – and even dealing with the occasional disagreement. It happens and it's all part of friendship and being human!

WHAT WOULD YOU DO?
A get-to-know-you game

Dec: How well do you know your friends?

Ant: Dec, I know **YOU** better than you know yourself! I know your favourite crisps are cheese and onion, you wear lucky socks when you watch Newcastle games, and your favourite person in the whole wide world is Ant McPartlin.

Dec: Er, yeah, OK. Anyway, where was I? Oh yeah, how well do you know your friends? You might already know their middle name or their best subject at school...

LUCKY SOCKS

Ant: Yours are Joseph Oliver and Maths.

Dec: But do you know what they'd do if they woke up and suddenly knew how to fly?

Ant: I think YOU would fly straight off on holiday. Can I come? You could give me a flying piggyback...

Dec: Shhhh! Here's a quiz to help you get to know your friends even better. It might lead to longer chats or silly answers. So – use your imagination and have fun!

HOW TO PLAY:

STEP 1:

You and your friend need a piece of paper each.
Draw a line down the middle of the page to make
two columns.

STEP 2:

Write your name at the top of the
first column and your friend's name
at the top of the second column.
(Your friend must do the same.)
Write the numbers 1 to 10 down
the left-hand side of each column.

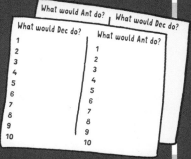

STEP 3:

For each question (see pages 38–9), write what
YOU would do in your column, then guess what
your friend would do and write it in their column.
Your friend must do the same on their paper.

STEP 4:

Time to share answers.
No peeking ahead of time!

**TURN OVER
TO PLAY . . .**

WHAT WOULD YOU DO?
Questions

1. You are about to perform in a talent show. What is your act?

2. You have invented a time machine. Where would you travel to?

3. You have the power to speak to animals. Which animal would you speak to first – and what would you say?

4. You are in charge of choosing a new sport for the Olympics. What would you choose?

5. You can only eat one type of food for the rest of your life. What would it be?

6. You have discovered a dusty old book of magic spells. What is the first spell you'd cast?

7. You are late to school. What is your perfect excuse going to be?

MY PET PIRANHA ATE MY HOMEWORK!

8. You get to meet your favourite celebrity or icon. Who would it be?

9. You can change one thing about the world (just one!). What would it be?

10. OMG – suddenly you are famous! What would you be famous for?

ANT'S TOP TIP: You can play with more than one friend – you just need more columns!

TURN OVER TO FIND OUT SOME OF ANT & DEC'S ANSWERS!

WHAT WOULD YOU DO?
Ant vs Dec

1. **You are about to perform in a talent show. What is your act?**

Ant: Dec would do Irish dancing while singing show tunes.

Dec: No chance! I'd breakdance while saying one of my favourite catchphrases: 'Evening, Prime Minister.'

Ant: Sounds great! What would I do?

Dec: A TV double act with your breakdancing, catchphrase-loving best mate?

Ant: No, thanks! I'd do a dog assault course with my pet pooches Milo, Bumble and Hurley — while rapping!

2. **You have invented a time machine. Where would you travel to?**

Ant: What's your guess for me?

Dec: You'd go back to Roman times, because you love ancient history — and you look great in a toga!

Ant: Thanks! Actually I would go everywhere! I'm a massive fan of history! Medieval King Ant! Pharaoh Ant! Want to hear my guess for you?

Dec: Go for it!

Ant: You'd go forward in time to see what we'll look like as old men!

Dec: Wrong! I'd go back to 1927, when Newcastle United last won the league!

3. **You have the power to speak to animals. Which animal would you speak to first – and what would you say?**

Ant: That's easy. As you're scared of birds, you'd speak to every single bird in the world to tell them to keep away from you!

Dec: Not a bad idea. But I'd actually speak to my dog. And **YOU** would also speak to your dogs! In that awful 'dog voice' you do …

Ant: Correct! I'm always talking to my dogs, but they never seem to understand me, **EVEN** when I put on my special and very cool 'dog voice'.

DID I RUFFLE SOME FEATHERS?

THE POWER OF KINDNESS

Kindness is more than just being nice. When you use your power of kindness, you're making a decision to do or say something **thoughtful** or **considerate** to help someone else. When you're kind, it makes others feel noticed and valued.

Ant: What's your favourite way of being kind, Dec?

Dec: If someone's feeling down, I always ask if they'd like a hug.

Ant: Your hugs *are* great!

Dec: What about you, Ant?

Ant: I'll pick up the phone if I think someone might need a chat. Although I always dial their number after I pick up the phone — just picking up the phone would be useless ...

BEING KIND MAKES YOU FEEL GOOD!

In fact, acts of kindness make the world a better place for everyone.

ACTIVATE YOUR POWER OF KINDNESS

Kick off your power of kindness in just one minute. Choose **THREE** things to do that will make someone's day. Remember, even the smallest acts of kindness can make a big difference!

HERE ARE SOME EXAMPLES . . .

HELP A FAMILY MEMBER
Offer to lend a hand with a chore or task.

GIVE A FRIEND A COMPLIMENT
Maybe you like something they're wearing or you're impressed with something they said in class.

GIVE SOMEONE A SMALL THING THAT YOU THINK THEY MIGHT APPRECIATE
Send a postcard to your nanna or ask an adult to help you bake her some cookies.

DEC'S TOP TIP: You don't even have to know someone to be kind to them. Just smiling at someone new at school or saying a big 'THANK YOU' to the bus driver counts!

ARGUMENTS CAN BE AWESOME

Ant: Have you ever had an argument with someone? We certainly have — it's perfectly normal for us two to have a little disagreement.

Dec: No, it isn't.

Ant: Yes, it is.

Dec: Fine! How about we agree to disagree?

Ant: I don't agree with doing that either.

Dec: Oh, forget it!

Ant: Not only is this normal, but arguing can actually be a good thing!

Dec: Now that, I *do* agree with.

Ant: Arguments can actually be really helpful. It's OK to disagree — here's why . . .

Arguments can lead to compromise.

Maybe you want to go to the cinema, but your friend wants to play football. Neither of you is 'wrong' – you just have different opinions. This is a great opportunity to compromise: maybe your friend picks what you do this time, and you choose next time?

Arguments can lead to positive change.

If you've done something that has upset your friend, encourage them to explain how they feel and why. Now you have a chance to change that behaviour and to say **"I'M SORRY"**.

If you're the one who's been upset by something, try to explain how you feel as calmly and kindly as you can. Then if your friend apologises to you, it's your chance to tell them that

YOU FORGIVE THEM.

TURN OVER FOR MORE TOP TIPS.

Working through an argument strengthens your relationship.

If you take the time to listen to each other, it shows that you care and want to understand each other better. Remember, while arguments are normal, it's important to move past them!

Walk away if the argument is getting out of hand.

Some people find arguments difficult and find it hard to see other people's point of view. Every now and then, when people are frustrating us, it's better to walk away – arguing with them might make the situation worse. Often when we give people time they will calm down, and friendships can be healed. Try to be patient with people.

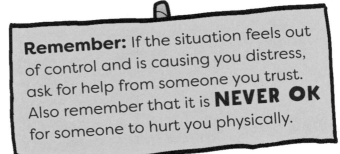

Remember: If the situation feels out of control and is causing you distress, ask for help from someone you trust. Also remember that it is **NEVER OK** for someone to hurt you physically.

FANTASTIC FRIENDS

My friends are always there when I need them.

Henry, age 8

My friends look out for me.

Eloise, age 10

My favourite thing about my friends is that everyone's unique and everyone has special talents they can share.

Cora, age 7

I'm happy when I am with my friends and family.

Scarlett, age 9

BESTIE BINGO

Playing Bestie Bingo is a great way to keep track of the adventures you have with your friends.

Ant: There are so many things us two like to do together — watch football, host live television shows, you know, the usual stuff...

Dec: Spending time with your bestie can boost your confidence and make you feel calmer. It's good for both of you — and it's lots of fun too!

HOW TO PLAY:

STEP 1:

Create two 16-square bingo card grids – one each for you and your bestie. Copy the one below or create your own.

STEP 2:

Put one challenge in each square.

HERE ARE SOME EXAMPLES . . .

MAKE PAPER AEROPLANES AND SEE WHOSE FLIES THE FURTHEST!

ONE OF YOU HAS TO KEEP A STRAIGHT FACE WHILE THE OTHER ONE TRIES TO MAKE THEM LAUGH. **No tickling though!**

RE-ENACT A SCENE FROM YOUR FAVOURITE MOVIE OR TV SHOW.

DRAW A PICTURE OF EACH OTHER WHILE WEARING BLINDFOLDS.

MAKE A DEN. **You could even sleep in it if your grown-ups agree!**

CREATE A COMIC WHERE YOU ARE BOTH SUPERHEROES. **(Or supervillains!)**

STEP 3:

Every time you do something together, cross off the square. When you've crossed off four in a row – in any direction – shout as loud as you can:

"BINGO!"

ANT'S TOP TIP: Why not surprise a friend with a Bestie Bingo card you've made specially for them!

WE CHALLENGE YOU

Surprise a friend

Doing something unexpected for a friend is a fun way to use your creativity. It will also make your friend feel great!

Ant: We surprise each other all the time. Last week I surprised Dec with a lovely present: a bucket and a big sponge.

Dec: I don't want to sound ungrateful, but why did you get me that?

Ant: Because tomorrow, I've got another big surprise for you.

Dec: Ooh, I love surprises! What is it?

Ant: You're going to spend all day washing my car with your brand-new sponge and bucket! **SURPRISE!**

Dec: Er, Ant, we need to talk about your definition of 'surprise'...

HOW CAN YOU SURPRISE A FRIEND? HERE ARE SOME IDEAS . . .

Silly surprise

Write down a joke or draw a funny picture.
Put it somewhere your friend will come across it
unexpectedly, like inside one of their books.

What's wrong?

I'M HOT CHOCOLATE!

Tasty surprise

Show up with your friend's favourite treat
or drink. You could even decorate the bag or cup!

Thoughtful surprise

Make a card or scrapbook of messages from
other friends or members of their family. They'll
be touched to find so many notes in one place!

Sporty surprise

Does your friend have a favourite sports team?
Surprise them by wearing that team's colours
when you watch the game together!

YOU OR ME?

A knowledge game

Who owns the most pairs of socks? Who would win in a thumb war? Grab a friend and play this super silly game!

HOW TO PLAY:

Ask a question, then both close your eyes and point to who you think it is – you or your friend. Open your eyes. Are you pointing to the same person?

1. **Who is the messiest?**

   Ant: Definitely Dec.

   Dec: What did you say? I can't hear you from under this pile of dirty clothes!

2. **Who gets up earlier in the mornings?**

   Ant: Dec!

   Dec: Me. I have a special alarm clock – my daughter!

3. **Who is the best breakdancer?**

   Ant: Me!

   Dec: Me! Right, that's it ... dance-off!

4. Who is the most dramatic?

Dec: Ant! He once got cross because I took too long brushing my teeth!

Ant: Dec! He once got bitten by a tiny spider in Australia and he pretended to faint.

5. Who loves chips the most?

Ant & Dec: That one's definitely a draw!

6. Who would build the best sandcastle?

Dec: Ant, he's more practical than me!

Ant: Me! I'm the king of the (sand) castle!

7. Who would be best at fighting off an army of mutant space monkeys?

Ant: I'd throw Dec at them and run away.

Dec: What? No! Please don't leave me with the mutant space monkeys!

8. Who is most likely to adopt a penguin?

Ant & Dec: We'd adopt a penguin together, of course!

I SUPPORT YOU

We all have moments when life feels tough. Being friends means being there for each other – for the good times . . . and the bad. Sometimes your friend will need someone to lean on. Sometimes it may be you who needs support.

Ant: If one of us gets down, we always know we can talk to the other one.

Dec: And that will often make us feel better.

HOW CAN YOU HELP A FRIEND WHO'S HAVING A HARD TIME?

YOUR TURN

Find a quiet place to ask if they're OK
Try and find somewhere private, away from other people. It's harder to open up in a crowd.

Listen
Remind your friend that you're there for them – and then listen. You don't always need to try and solve your friend's problems. Sometimes the most powerful thing is giving them someone to talk to.

It's OK not to talk!

Maybe your friend doesn't feel ready to open up – and that's OK! It doesn't mean they don't value you as a friend. Just knowing that you're there to support them is important.

Take their mind off it

Sometimes you can help by talking about something else to cheer them up or doing an activity you both enjoy.

You don't have to do it on your own

If your friend's problems are very serious, you can help your friend speak to an adult they trust or talk to Childline (see page 160).

Ant: It means everything to know Dec is there for me, no matter what.

Dec: I feel so lucky that I can tell Ant anything and talk to him at any time.

WE CHALLENGE YOU

Life swap

Have you ever wondered what it would be like to swap lives with a friend for a day? Why not give it a go! Here's the best part – it's great for your friendship because you each get to focus on what makes the other special!

Doing a life swap should be a bit of a laugh, so make sure you're both comfortable with everything. Pick a day when there isn't something more important going on – and don't forget to make sure your parents or guardians agree!

HOW CAN YOU SWAP LIVES WITH A FRIEND?

Swap interests

Is your friend always singing their favourite song? You're going to need to learn it too!

Ant: This means I'll have to sing loads of songs from musicals ...

Dec: Can't wait to hear that!

Swap catchphrases

"Seriously?" "I can't even!" Whatever your friend is known for saying, make sure to use it – **LOTS**!

Ant: The voting is noooooow open.

Dec: Hey, that's my line!

Swap styles

What does your friend wear most? Jeans and a T-shirt? Dungarees? A hat? Try dressing like them – use your creativity to get as close as you can!

Copycat snacks

What does your friend like to eat? Why not try choosing the same or similar things. Do they really, really, really like broccoli? Give it a go!

Ant: What've you got for lunch, Dec?

Dec: A cheese and ham toastie, a bag of cheese and onion crisps, and an apple. How about you?

Ant: I would never eat that stuff! Mine is a pizza, topped with ham, cheese, onion and apple.

Dec: What?! Copycat!

HAVE FUN – AND DON'T FORGET TO SWAP BACK!

THE POWER OF EMPATHY

Everyone is different. We think and feel in different ways. Using empathy means putting yourself in someone else's shoes to imagine how they're feeling.

Ant: When Dec and I first met, we were both child actors in a TV show called *Byker Grove*.

Dec: I'd been there for a while when Ant arrived, so I knew everyone — but he was the **'NEW BOY'**.

Ant: A new boy with a very cool collection of baseball caps...

Dec: I knew that being the new boy wasn't easy, so I chatted to Ant and tried to make him feel at home.

Ant: That Christmas, I sent Dec a Fred Flintstone card asking if he wanted to go to the football with me. And we became best friends! But it all started because Dec showed empathy. Do you feel good about that, Dec?

Dec: Yes, I **YABBA-DABBA DO**!

ACTIVATE YOUR POWER OF EMPATHY

Time to activate your power of empathy in just one minute. Choose **THREE** ways to reach out to someone else and show them you're trying to understand their perspective.

HERE ARE SOME EXAMPLES . . .

ASK A FRIEND HOW THEY'RE FEELING, AND REALLY LISTEN.

PAY ATTENTION TO SOMEONE'S BODY LANGUAGE. Are they smiling or frowning? Are they breathing heavily or do they seem relaxed? How do you think they're feeling?

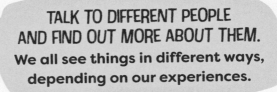

TALK TO DIFFERENT PEOPLE AND FIND OUT MORE ABOUT THEM. We all see things in different ways, depending on our experiences.

How did using your empathy superpower make you feel? Can you think of times when you've been treated with empathy by others? How did it feel?

MAKING NEW FRIENDS

It isn't always easy to make new friends. But we can all do it, if we try! What's the secret? It starts with taking the plunge . . . and talking!

It all starts with "hello!"
Introduce yourself and make eye contact. Don't forget to smile!

Look for something you have in common
Maybe you're in the same class. Maybe you play the same sport or like the same video games. Maybe you have exactly the same number of noses!

Find something to share
You could offer to share a snack. You could even share a favourite video or song.

Try an ice-breaker
Ice-breaker questions are a great way to start a conversation. Your questions could be silly or serious – either way, you'll definitely learn interesting things!

HERE ARE SOME ICE-BREAKERS TO GET YOU STARTED . . .

1. If you could travel through time, where would you go and why?

2. What is the last thing you watched on TV or YouTube?

3. What's your favourite joke?

What's a crocodile's favourite game?

SNAP!

4. If it started to rain slime right now, what would you do?

5. If you could form a double act with anyone in the world, who would it be and why?

6. If you had to do a Bushtucker Trial, would you rather eat an eyeball, or get covered in fish guts?

Remember: Sometimes the other person may not want to say hello back. **THAT'S OK**. You did your best and don't let that put you off talking to the next person!

ANT'S BRILLI-ANT JOKES

Who makes you laugh? Who laughs hardest at your jokes? Sharing a laugh is a great way to connect with friends – including ones you've just met.

Dec: Laughter is really important to us. We make each other laugh all the time. Sometimes when we don't even mean to!

Ant: Why not give your friends and family a giggle with these propa silly jokes. You'll find more on page 90–1!

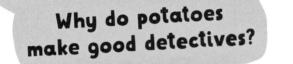

Why do potatoes make good detectives?

THEY ALWAYS KEEP THEIR EYES PEELED.

Why aren't eggs allowed to tell jokes?

BECAUSE THEY'D CRACK EACH OTHER UP.

KNOCK, KNOCK.

Who's there?
ANT.
Ant who?
<u>ANT</u> YOU GLAD I CAME OVER!

What do you call a bunch of spy ducks?

CODE-QUACKERS.

What do you call a fish wearing a bow tie?

SO<u>FISH</u>TICATED.

What's a pirate's favourite subject in school?

ARRRRRRT.

63

WHAT TYPE OF FRIEND ARE YOU?

Ant: There are loads of great ways to be a supportive friend.

Dec: We're the kind of friends who always have each other's backs and know each other like the back of our hands.

Ant: For instance, we're very good at finishing each other's ...

Dec: Sandwiches.

Ant: Sentences.

Dec: Oh. Right. Like a lot of friends, what makes us laugh the most is when something silly happens to the other one. Once we were walking up some stairs at ITV and the handrails had just been painted. Ant didn't see **ANY** of the 'Wet Paint' signs and grabbed the handrail, covering his hand in bright blue paint! That is still the funniest thing I've ever seen in my entire life.

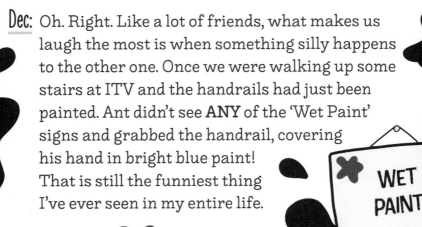

Ant: It was funny — but not as funny as when we were pop stars and Dec tried to dye his hair blond. He was in the bathroom for ages. Eventually, he came out and his hair was bright red!

THE GUINEA PIGS OF STYLE

Dec: But there's another important thing to know about us. When you're as close as we are, nothing's off limits. We've given ourselves permission to laugh at each other.

Ant: But we would never laugh at someone we'd just met because that would be unkind.

Dec: The point is that we love each other really. That's what makes it so funny.

Ant: So what about you and your friends? What kind of friends are you?

TURN OVER TO TAKE A FRIENDSHIP QUIZ AND FIND OUT!

WHAT TYPE OF FRIEND ARE YOU? Quiz

1. **When you meet up with your friends, what's your favourite thing to do?**

a) Volunteer somewhere to help people.

b) Go to our favourite park and mess about.

c) Finish building an awesome Lego® spaceship.

d) Anything – so long as we're together!

2. **When you meet someone new at school, how do you start chatting with them?**

a) Ask them about their hobbies.

b) Think of an activity, then invite them along.

c) Sing them a song about smelly feet.

d) Ask them how they like their new school.

3. **What is the biggest thing you and your friends have in common?**

a) We have similar opinions.

b) We share the same sense of humour.

c) We love multiple-choice friendship quizzes.

d) Practically everything!

4. Your friend shows up at your house one night and tells you their family have been replaced by evil space robots! What do you do?

   a) Lend them your book called *How to Defeat Evil Space Robots*.

   b) Go round and tell the robots your best jokes . . . if there's one thing evil space robots can't fight, it's the power of laughter!

   c) Jump in your Lego® spaceship and travel with them to the furthest galaxy to capture the Power Crystal that controls the robots.

   d) Invite your friend to move in and live with you.

5. But seriously . . . your friend tells you they're being picked on. What do you do first?

   a) Advise them to talk to a trusted adult.

   b) Think of something fun to cheer them up and show them you care about them.

   c) Stand up for them – go to the bullies and tell them to stop.

   d) Give them a hug and ask how they're feeling.

TURN OVER AND SEE WHAT TYPE OF FRIEND YOU ARE!

WHAT TYPE OF FRIEND ARE YOU? Quiz answers

IF YOU ANSWERED . . .

Mostly As

You're a helpful friend!

You are responsible, practical and full of wonderful ideas. You always look out for your mates and give great advice.

And remember, you don't always need to have the answers to be a great friend. Sometimes the best thing is to listen!

Mostly Bs

You're a fun friend!

You are warm-hearted and energetic. You make even the most boring situations fun just by being there. You can make anyone laugh – especially your best friend!

And remember, it's OK to be serious sometimes. You don't always have to be the fun one.

Mostly Cs

You're an adventurous friend!

You love being out and about, and trying new things. You are great at coming up with activities to do with your friends, and you know just how to make people feel good about themselves.

And remember, you don't always have to go on an adventure to have a good time with your friends. Sometimes it's important to chill out and take it easy together!

Mostly Ds

You're a caring friend!

You are loyal and are there for your friends, no matter what. You are kind and compassionate, and always in tune with how your friends are feeling. You're everyone's shoulder to cry on.

And remember, make sure you take the time to look after YOU as well. It's OK to put yourself first sometimes.

FRIENDLY FACES
Create a bestie portrait

Do you like to draw? Follow these six steps to create a portrait of you and your bestie that you can give them as a gift or keep in your own special space.

You'll need:
- Paper
- Coloured pens
- A friend!

STEP 1:

Draw a big rectangle at the bottom of the paper.

STEP 2:

Draw a lowercase letter 'm' on top of the rectangle.

STEP 3:

Now add two sets of eyes! Add the pupils so they're looking at each other. And don't forget to add bestie smiles!

STEP 4:

Add arms and hair. If you like wearing hats, you can draw them on too!

STEP 5:

Draw lines for your T-shirts. You can colour these in your favourite colours, or add a design!

Dec: When I'm drawing Ant, I make sure the forehead is nice and big.

Ant: He's right – it's my best feature!

STEP 6:

Finally, write your names in the rectangle below your portraits, and add in a message if you like.

Remember: You don't have to draw just one friend. Add **ALL YOUR FRIENDS** if you want to!

WOULD YOU RATHER?
Quiz

Challenge a friend or family member to play this silly game!

HOW TO PLAY:

Count the number of times you have the same answer and the number of times you have a different answer.

1. Would you rather have a cat or a dog as a pet?

2. If you had to pick one type of breakfast to eat FOR EVER, would you rather have cereal or toast?

3. Would you rather spend the night in a haunted house or a spider-filled jungle?

4. If you could only have pizza OR chips for ever, which would you rather have?

5. Would you rather ONLY be able whisper in a teeny tiny voice OR be able to shout in a very loud voice?

6. **Would you rather have the power of invisibility or be able to fly?**

7. **Would you rather go to space or travel to the centre of the Earth?**

8. **Would you rather be incredible at singing or amazing at sport?**

9. **Would you rather come face to face with 100 elephants the size of a spider or a spider the size of an elephant?**

10. **Would you rather watch Ant doing art with an aardvark or Dec doing a dance-off with a dodo?**

Ant: This is getting VERY weird. Dodos are extinct.

Dec: And aardvarks are terrible artists.

Ant: Apart from that, it's a great question.

THE DISCO DODO

THIS WAY TO FIND OUT MORE!

WOULD YOU RATHER?
Quiz answers

IF YOU ANSWERED MOSTLY THE SAME WAY . . .

You have loads in common, which gives you lots to talk about and lots of fun things to do together!

IF YOU ANSWERED MOSTLY DIFFERENTLY . . .

You each bring different things to your friendship. That means you can share your hobbies and interests and learn new things!

SOMEWHERE IN THE MIDDLE . . .

You have some similarities and some differences. You share lots of interests and you can also inspire each other with new stuff!

Remember: You might have just a few friends or lots and lots. It really doesn't matter. What counts is that your friends are there for you!

BRILLIANT BESTIES

My best friend makes me laugh all the time. We have a lot of things in common!

Megan, age 10

My best friend cares about other people.

Dila, age 10

My best friend is always smiling and she is happy for me when I achieve something.

Emel, age 10

What makes YOU FEEL AMAZING?

THE PUG OF PAMPERING

CHAPTER 3

FIND YOUR HAPPY

Take a few minutes to sit and think about what your favourite thing to do is. Really think. What makes you fizz with happiness? What makes you feel amazing? OK . . . now do more of it! Want to improve at a hobby? Set yourself some goals. What new skill would you like to try? Ask friends, family or teachers to help you give it a go! This chapter is all about finding what makes **YOU** happy, and giving yourself new challenges that will power your positivity!

WHAT DO YOU <u>LOVE</u> DOING?

Did you know that doing something you enjoy every day actually helps you stay healthy and happy? Laughing and having fun decreases stress hormones and increases immune cells and infection-fighting antibodies.

Dec: What's your favourite thing to do, Ant?

Ant: Ooh, good question. Playing football, spending time with my dogs and...

Dec: Hanging out with me?

Ant: I was going to say "Feeding fish eyes to celebrities" — but yeah, yours works too.

Dec: So what makes **YOU**, our lovely reader, happy?

Ant: Like, really happy...?

THE COSY CUPCAKE LOVES READING CLASSIC COMEDIES

YOUR TURN

Why not make a list of things you love doing? It could be hobbies, spending time with friends, maths homework . . . Add as much detail as you like, whether it's 'football' or 'doing celebrity impressions with my bestie and laughing till we cry'. Keep hold of your list to use on page 85.

Ant: How about 'Playing football while doing celebrity impressions?' Imagine it — 'I'm going to take this penalty while talking like SpongeBob SquarePants.'

Dec: If that's what you enjoy, write it down!

Now ask yourself how you feel when you do things you love. Calm? Excited? Confident? Creative?

How do you think other people see you when you're doing things you love? You could ask friends and family: **"What am I like to be around when I'm doing my hobby?"**

I like movie nights with snacks because you watch movies with your family. And I dance at the end!

Ismaeel, age 6

EXTRAORDINARY HOBBIES
What could YOU try?

So you've heard of baking, singing, vlogging and sports – but what about more unusual hobbies? What could you try right now? What would you like to have a go at one day?

Ant: I would love to do a skydive, but I can never find the time.

Dec: And I would love to water ski, but I can't.

Ant: Because you can never find the time?

Dec: No. Sharks.

Ant: I feel like we're getting off the point. How about **YOU** give some unusual hobbies a go? You might surprise yourself!

Bucket drumming

This is a popular street art – and a fun way to work on your percussion skills. Turn an old plastic bucket upside-down and it becomes a musical instrument!

Stone skipping

This is the sport of throwing a flat stone across the water and seeing how many times it bounces. Did you know that there is the World Stone Skipping Championships? The world record is 88 skips!

Word collecting

A sesquipedalian *(sess-kwi-peh-day-lee-an)* is a person who loves using long words – who knew? Why not collect your own weird and wonderful words and write them down on cards or in a notebook. Here are some of our favourites:

BUMFUZZLING
(adjective): confusing

YITTEN
(adjective): frightened

ARGLE-BARGLE
(noun): a stream of nonsense

What are YOUR favourite things to do?
Is there a hobby that involves these things? Why not challenge yourself to find out more!

THE POWER OF CREATIVITY

Creativity is more than just being good at art or having a great singing voice. Being creative means coming up with new ideas, solving problems and imagining new things.

Ant: I've got **SO** many ideas for great new inventions!

Dec: Ant, we haven't got time to talk about your idea for a chocolate teapot...

Ant: I'm telling you, it's a winner.

ANYONE FOR TEA?

Creativity allows you to express yourself, through art, writing, acting, dancing or building things.

Don't be afraid to try something new:

THE BEST PART ABOUT BEING CREATIVE IS THAT ANYTHING GOES.

ACTIVATE YOUR POWER OF **CREATIVITY**

Celebrate your power of creativity! Try these **THREE** creative challenges – or come up with your own.

HERE ARE SOME EXAMPLES . . .

THE BIRTHDAY BUNNY

CREATE

Make a birthday card for a friend – without using paper! Will you use a leaf? A rock? An old T-shirt? Or maybe all you need is your body to create a singing- and-dancing birthday message?

BUILD

What is the most spectacular boat that you can build using only things that you can find in your bedroom? Bonus: ask an adult if you can try floating your boat in a sink of water!

IMAGINE

Imagine there's a lightning storm and you lose power. What would you do for light? How could you cook food? What other problems might need solving?

WE CHALLENGE YOU

Try something new

New experiences are good for us. Even if it seems strange or scary at first, doing something new can often be a really positive experience!

Ant: We try new things for TV shows all the time. Twenty years ago, we tried making a live TV show in Australia. The show had the longest title in the history of television and it involved making celebrities do **REALLY** gross stuff.

Dec: We were nervous and we weren't sure it would work … but it did! We've also tried tons of new things for *Saturday Night Takeaway* — we've Riverdanced, played in a vegetable orchestra, sung sea shanties and been driven around in a golf buggy by Lewis Hamilton!

Ant: The point is, these were all new things that we were nervous about doing, but which made us feel really good in the end.

ARE YOU READY TO TRY SOMETHING NEW?

Challenge your body

When you try a new physical skill, it builds hand-eye coordination and boosts concentration. The more you do it, the better you'll get! Why not try dancing or juggling?

Challenge your mind

A workout for your brain! You could go to a class, use books or an app to develop a skill. Why not try coding or learning British Sign Language?

Old hobby, new twist

The next time you choose a book, pick a different type. For example, if you love reading fantasy stories, maybe try a non-fiction book or a whodunnit instead? Ask a friend what they're reading to get some inspiration!

Swapsies

Did you make a list on page 79? Try swapping it with a friend. You try out their favourite things and they get to experience the things that you enjoy!

ANT'S TOP TIP: Did you try something new, but didn't like it? That's OK! Thinking about why you didn't like it gives you useful clues about other things that you might *actually* like doing.

HOW TO MAKE
a comedy sketch

Want to try something new but can't think of what to try? Asking friends and family what they enjoy doing is a great way to find out about new activities.

Ant: One of the things we love doing is creating the sketches we do on TV — we get to dress up, pretend to be other people, sing songs **AND** tell jokes.

HA! HA!

Dec: Sometimes they go well, sometimes they don't — and that can be even funnier!

Ant: Once we did a sketch with singer Jess Glynne where we both kept falling off a giant wall!

Dec: We also surprised Ed Sheeran and got him to play the trumpet. We put boot polish on the end of the trumpet, so his lips turned black!

HA! HA!

WHY NOT GIVE IT A GO?

Creating sketches is a great way to use your creativity. You could do it on your own or with friends. Maybe it's just a quick sketch or maybe it becomes a performance with costumes and everything.

HERE ARE SOME TOP TIPS FOR GETTING STARTED . . .

Create strong characters

Make sure you've got easy-to-recognise characters – for example, a medieval queen and a court jester, or a superhero and their arch-nemesis. They can be from any time or place you like – the only limit is your imagination!

Think of a story with a beginning . . .

A good way to start is to give one character a secret that the other one doesn't know about. For instance, the jester has lost the queen's crown.

. . . a middle . . .

Then give the other character something they really, really want – maybe the queen urgently needs her crown to wear to her birthday party.

. . . and an ending

Finally, you need an ending. What solution will the jester come up with? Does he make the queen a new crown out of toilet paper and hope she doesn't notice? Does the queen tickle the jester until he tells her the truth? Does the jester's dog turn up wearing the crown?

HA! HA!

TURN OVER FOR MORE TIPS.

Go with the flow (or the script!)

You could write a script **OR** you can make it up as you go along – this is called 'improvising'. It's a great way to come up with stuff that will surprise your friends and make them laugh.

Dec: We do this all the time on *I'm a Celebrity ... Get Me Out of Here*!

Make it physical

Do something physical! Wear funny clothes, use a funny voice, pretend to trip over – anything you like!

Watch it back

HA! HA! HA!

Use a phone or other device to film you and your friends practising – then watch it back and see what's funny and what's not.

Ant: We always do this when we rehearse 'The End of the Show Show' – we practise all week and watch what we've done to try and improve.

HA! HA!

Get an audience

Convince your family, guardian or friends to watch you – hearing people laugh will tell you which bits are the funniest.

Ant: When we hear the audience laugh on *Saturday Night Takeaway*, it's the best feeling ever.

Say "It's OK" to nerves!

Don't worry if you get nervous before you perform – it's normal. And of course, if you don't want to go through with a performance, you don't have to.

Dec: Believe it or not, we still get nervous **EVERY** Saturday night!

Finally – and most importantly – feel free to ignore **ALL** this advice! If you and your friends just want to mess about and make each other laugh, **GO FOR IT**!

THE ONLY RULES ARE BE SAFE AND HAVE FUN!

HA! HA!

MORE BRILLI-ANT JOKES

Ant: We promised more jokes …

Dec: And we were serious. We're very, very serious about jokes.

Ant: That's confusing. Let's just tell the jokes!

What is the tallest building in the world?

A LIBRARY – IT HAS THE MOST STORIES.

What do you call a troll who gets full marks in every test?

AN OGRE-ACHIEVER.

What's the spookiest thing to eat at a beach picnic?

SAND-WITCHES!

What do clams do on their birthdays?

SHELL-EBRATE.

What did the narwhal say to her sick friend?

GET WHALE SOON.

Why should you never do a maths test in the jungle?
THERE ARE TOO MANY CHEETAHS!

Why did the jellybean take an exam?

TO BECOME A SMARTIE!

PRACTICE MAKES PROGRESS

Getting really good at any hobby or skill can take lots of time and patience. No one – absolutely no one – is 'naturally talented'. It's a great feeling when we try hard, challenge ourselves and get better!

Ant: I'm really good at telling jokes. Here's one of my favourites.

> **Why did the sand blush?**

Dec: I don't know. Why did the sand blush?

> **BECAUSE THE SEA WEED.**

Dec: Ha ha ha ha! That's the funniest thing I've ever heard in my entire life!

Ant: Thanks. What are you really good at, Dec?

Dec: I'm a brilliant actor.

Ant: What? When was the last time you did any brilliant acting?

Dec: Three seconds ago, when I laughed at your joke!

YOUR TURN

What's your favourite hobby – one you would like to improve at? Can you think of:

3 things you are great at

2 things you want to practise

1 thing you will try in order to challenge yourself.

Write a list, draw a mind map or make a video of yourself talking about them. For example:

My favourite hobby is: football

I'm great at: dribbling, passing, taking corners

I want to practise: penalty shots, scissor kicks

I will try: goalkeeping

Ant: Just say to yourself, "I'm like a doctor – I love patience!"

Dec: Sigh.

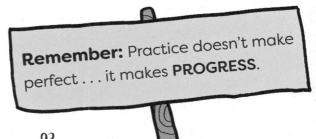

Remember: Practice doesn't make perfect . . . it makes **PROGRESS**.

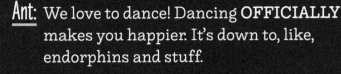

WE CHALLENGE YOU

Have a dance party!

Ant: We love to dance! Dancing **OFFICIALLY** makes you happier. It's down to, like, endorphins and stuff.

Dec: Thank you, Dr McPartlin.

Ant: You're welcome! But seriously, dancing is a great way to get moving and have a giggle.

WHAT'S YOUR PERFECT DANCE PARTY?

Make it snappy!
Bust a move for 10 seconds. **WHY NOT?**

Pass it on!
Film your best moves and send it to your gran to put a smile on her face. You could challenge her to send you a video back.

THE DANCING
GRAN FLAN

PRAAAAAACTICE!

Are you and your mates good at thinking up moves? Try planning a whole routine for a song and rehearsing it. It's called 'choreography'. Now you can perform the dance whenever you hear the song . . . no matter where you are!

Spoof it!

Recreate your favourite dance video with your friends. Or . . . spoof it by dressing up as silly versions of the dancers and adding new moves of your own.

THE LIZARD
HIP-HOP TANGO

Mash-up moves!

So, you're great at matching awesome moves to a killer beat? How about picking a style that's **COMPLETELY** different from the music? Try doing a tango to a hip-hop beat – make it as silly and surprising as you can!

Be unique

Invent a move. Give it a name. Teach it to your friends. It might be the next big dance craze!

WHY MISTAKES CAN BE MARVELLOUS

Everyone makes mistakes. It's part of being human. In order to learn, grow and challenge ourselves, we NEED to make mistakes!

Ant: Us two are no different.

Dec: For instance, we once got into a giant hot-air balloon to film *Britain's Got Talent*. No one could hear us talking above the noise of the fire thing-y bit in the balloon. Oops!

Ant: And then we, er, crash landed in the middle of someone's garden. But, like with all mistakes, we learnt a valuable lesson.

Dec: What was it again?

Ant: Don't go up in hot-air balloons to film *Britain's Got Talent*!

Dec: Oh, yeah. I think there's a valuable life lesson for everyone there. But seriously, without mistakes, we never discover new things ...

THE HOT-AIR BABOON

YOUR TURN

CAN YOU THINK OF A MISTAKE YOU HAVE MADE?

HOW DID IT MAKE YOU FEEL?

WHAT DID YOU LEARN FROM IT?

WHAT WOULD YOU DO DIFFERENTLY NEXT TIME?

NEXT TIME YOU MAKE A MISTAKE, TELL YOURSELF THIS IS OK:

I CAN **LEARN** FROM **THIS MISTAKE.**

I CAN MAKE PROGRESS.

Remember: Making a mistake doesn't mean you have failed. It is an important part of building 'resilience'. You can find more information on page 112.

WE CHALLENGE YOU

Dare to prepare

Ant: We both love football. We love playing it, watching it — we even recorded a song about it once! But before we play, it's important to warm up our bodies. We do that by . . .

Dec: Putting on massive coats.

Ant: No, by doing stretches!

Dec: Oh, yeah!

Ant: It's the same when we're going on TV. We always do a vocal warm-up to get our voices ready. One of our favourites is this tongue-twister:

A BOX OF BISCUITS, A BOX OF MIXED BISCUITS, AND A BISCUIT MIXER.

Ant: Best of all, you get to laugh at your friend making a mess of it, which is the part of the warm-up that helps us relax!

THE TONGUE-TIED CHAMELEON →

YOUR TURN

Everyone gets nervous before doing something important, like a test, sports match or performance. Warm-ups are a great way to soothe nerves and prepare your mind and body to do your best! Try these warm-ups on your own, in pairs or in a group.

Simon/Simone says

You know the game Simon Says
– well, it's great for warm-ups!
Pick a leader who calls instructions
such as "Simon says do star jumps",
which you all have to do – except when
the leader *doesn't* say "Simon says".

It's as easy as A, B, C

Go through the alphabet
from A to Z. For each letter, pick an object.
Now you pretend to be that object – and don't forget to include sound effects!

Sky writing

Imagine your finger is a pencil and use it to write your name in the air. Add a flourish or put a big circle around it . . . whatever feels good. Now do the same with your other hand, then your elbow, knee, foot, and even your tongue. **EVERYONE** is going to look very, VERY silly!

MY BIG DREAMS

Whatever your dreams are, here are some things to remember . . . Your dreams are awesome. Your dreams matter. Your dreams may change the world.

Ant: We've been very lucky: a lot of our dreams have come true. We've worked hard, we've never let setbacks get us down and most importantly, we each had our best friend by our side.

Dec: We didn't always know we'd end up being a double act on TV though.

Ant: Nope. We started out as actors. Then we were pop stars. We didn't know it at the time, but those two things would be a big part of what we do now. On *Saturday Night Takeaway*, we dress up, play characters, and sing and dance — our early career turned out to be amazing preparation.

Dec: To make **YOUR** dreams come true, the first question is: what can you do **RIGHT NOW** that will help get you closer to your dream?

MY BIG DREAMS

1
2
3
4
5

YOUR TURN

Write it down

Writing lets you dream big – even bigger than saying it out loud. Now you're a step closer to bringing your dream to life!

Practise the word 'yet'

If you can't do something right now, it just means you aren't there *yet*. 'Yet' means "I'm still learning, and I'll keep trying". Achieving your dreams will take time. It will take effort. And you know what? That's great! You get to learn and have fun along the way.

DON'T RUSH IT!

Roll with change

Dreams are like the weather – they can change. And of course, they don't always come true. But that's not a reason to give up . . .

WHATEVER HAPPENS, KEEP ON DREAMING.

WE CHALLENGE YOU

Set a new goal

Setting goals gives us something to focus on and work towards – and it feels incredible when we achieve something new. If the thought of setting goals feels overwhelming right now, try practising self-care instead (see page 119). Wait until you feel like a challenge!

HOW CAN YOU SET A NEW GOAL?

Think of something you want to achieve. It could be a short-term goal, like planning a digital-free day. Or it could be a long-term goal, like saving up money or writing in your journal every day for a month.

FEED ME!

Work backwards

A goal is more than just a wish – it's planning the steps you need to make something a reality. Start with where you want to end up, then write down everything you need to do to get there.

Mini goals

If you're working towards a big goal, it's important to celebrate your progress along the way. Set some mini goals – each one is worth celebrating!

Tell your friends and family

We're all much more likely to achieve our goals if we say them aloud to friends and family – **AND** you'll have other people cheering you on!

Celebrate your success

Have you achieved your goal? Share the good news with your friends and family. And then write down: 'I achieved this goal!' and put it somewhere you'll see every day.

Keep up the good work

Once you've achieved a goal, it can be hard to motivate yourself to carry on practising. Stick with it! Maybe you need a new goal to help you move forward!

Ant: Even if you don't achieve every one of your goals, try to focus on what you learnt along the way. Be proud that you tried as hard as you could!

Dec: Maybe some of your goals will help you get closer to your dreams as well.

THE STICK OF
STICKING WITH IT

CHAPTER <u>4</u>

NOT FEELING IT?

Happy, sad, angry, confused . . .
Recognising our feelings is the most
important thing we can do to keep our
brains and bodies healthy. This chapter
is about finding ways to manage those
challenging feelings – and sharing
them with trusted others in a way that
feels safe, comfortable and right for
YOU. Write, draw or talk about them . . .
your feelings are important!

CHECKING IN ON YOU

Ant: I don't feel cheerful all the time.

Dec: Neither do I.

Ant: No one does. And **THAT'S OK**.

Dec: One of the great things about being best friends is that we don't have to put on a 'front' with each other if we're not feeling great. We don't have to pretend to be feeling something we're not.

Ant: Absolutely — and when I don't feel cheerful, it can be for all sorts of different reasons — maybe I'm worried about someone I love, maybe work isn't going well, maybe I just feel a bit down.

Dec: We've always been close, but we're so much closer than we used to be because we're honest and open about our feelings.

THE CHEETAH OF CHECKING IN →

Ant: And it's not just each other we talk to. We have our families and other friends that we can confide in ... if we feel like talking.

Dec: And if we don't feel like talking, that's fine too – sometimes we just need some time and space to be left alone.

Ant: Yes, the important thing is to recognise how you're feeling and decide how you want to deal with it, otherwise you just bottle things up.

Dec: So, check in with yourself, ask for support if you need it – and remember, anything you're feeling now will probably change over time.

Ant: And most importantly ...

BE **KIND** TO YOURSELF!

Remember: Sometimes it might take time to figure out how you're feeling. The more you check in with yourself, the easier it will get.

MOOD SLEUTH
How are you really feeling?

HOW'S IT GOING?

IT'S GOING GREAT, THANK YOU.

"How's it going?" "All right?" "How are you?" We hear these questions **SO** often that sometimes we answer automatically without really thinking: how *am* I feeling?

It's important to stop and think about how you're really feeling, deep down. This can help stop feelings from building up inside and becoming difficult to manage.

ANT'S TOP TIP: Learn new words for feelings. You might start with 'angry', but what other 'feeling words' can you uncover?

108

HERE ARE SOME STEPS YOU CAN TAKE TO TUNE IN TO YOUR EMOTIONS . . .

STEP 1:

Take slow, deep breaths, in through your nose and out through your mouth. This helps quieten your mind and lets you focus on your feelings.

STEP 2:

Ask yourself: how am I feeling? Notice what feelings come to mind. Try to name the emotions. You could say them aloud or write them down.

STEP 3:

Tell yourself: it's OK to feel the way I do. Say this out loud or write it down.

STEP 4:

Ask yourself: what thoughts have caused me to feel the way I do? Identifying this can help your feelings become less overwhelming and easier to talk about.

STEP 5:

Ask yourself: what do I need? Make a list of anything that could help you move forward, for example speaking to a person who has upset you.

If you practise this every day, you'll find your detective skills getting better and better!

THOUGHT <u>OR</u> FACT?

Just because you think something, it doesn't make it true. If something is bothering you, it's important to take a step back to ask yourself: **is this a fact or is it a thought?** Noticing our thoughts and fact-checking them helps us to avoid making negative assumptions or jumping to conclusions.

LOOK AT THIS SCENE. WHICH ARE THOUGHTS AND WHICH ARE FACTS?

Try using this checklist to help you work out
what is a thought and what is a fact.

THOUGHT OR FACT CHECKLIST
Ask yourself:

- Is what I'm thinking definitely true?

- Is what I'm thinking likely to change?

- Could there be another way of looking at this?

- How does this thought make me feel?

- If this thought floated away, would it change how I'm feeling?

DOG IS WEARING A SKIRT.

I SAW CAT PRACTISING IN THE PARK EARLIER.

I DON'T THINK THE HEDGEHOG LIKES ME.

CAT IS RIDING A UNICYCLE.

RESILI-ANTS

IT'S OK TO ASK FOR HELP WHEN YOU NEED IT.

'Resilience' means overcoming difficult experiences and being able to say, "Yeah, I learned something from that." The good news is that we can all become more resilient, one small step at a time.

Ant: When we were 17 and starring in the children's drama *Byker Grove*, we were told that we were going to leave the show.

Dec: It's still one of the most difficult moments of our career — we loved the job and suddenly, it was gone.

Ant: We had to show resilience — and the fact we were both experiencing it together meant we could help each other get through it.

Dec: When you have tough moments like that, it's important to ask for help and get support from the people closest to you — just like we did.

TRY NEW THINGS, EVEN IF THEY SEEM STRANGE OR SCARY.

CHANGE HAPPENS ALL THE TIME. ACCEPTING CHANGE ALLOWS YOU TO GROW.

IT'S OK TO MAKE MISTAKES. YOU CAN LEARN FROM THEM!

Ant: Sometimes things happen that are tough to deal with — it's just a part of everyday life.

Dec: We've always learnt a lot more from the tougher moments than we have from the successes. But you don't have to listen to me. Why not listen to a wise, thoughtful **ANT**...

Ant: Aw, thanks, Dec.

Dec: Er, I meant these tiny cartoon ants...

Ant: I think what you're saying is **ALL** ants are wise and thoughtful?

Dec: Exactly!

Can you think of a time when YOU have learnt from a mistake? Or tried something new despite being nervous? Or shown courage by asking for help? **If so, you were showing your resilience!**

WOOHOO! YOU'RE A RESILI-ANT TOO!

MOOD-BOOSTERS
Feel-good activities for your body and brain

Everyone has bad days. Sometimes, challenging thoughts can spiral out of control and start to feel overwhelming. When this happens, try focusing on your body to help clear your head. Exercise can improve your mood and reduce anxiety.

HERE ARE SOME FUN CHALLENGES TO GET YOU STARTED . . .

Ant's keepy-uppys

Ask an adult to blow up a balloon. Now, using your hands and arms . . . and feet and legs . . . and head . . . try to keep the balloon off the ground. How long can you go for?

DON'T STOP TILL YOU POP!

ANT'S KEEPY-UPPY RECORD:
6 minutes, 21 seconds.

Running wild

Running is great for releasing tension. But don't stop there! Why not try skipping, hopping . . . or jogging backwards? (Carefully, of course!)

The chicken dance

Tap your head 8 times.
Tap your shoulders 8 times.
Tap your thighs 8 times.
Tap your knees 8 times.

Then go back through tapping everything 4 times. Then 2 times. Then 1 time. Finally . . . make your arms into wings and shout, **"CHICKEN!"** How quickly can you do all the moves?

DON'T KNOW THE MOVES? JUST WING IT!

The me tree

Stand on one leg and bend your other leg out to the side, resting your foot gently just below the knee of your straight leg. Raise your arms into the air. You are doing a yoga position called Tree Pose! Imagine your leg is a long root connecting you to the ground, your arms are branches reaching to the sky, and your chest is a strong trunk. Take deep breaths and use all your concentration to try not to wobble!

ASK YOURSELF: How does your body feel after doing one of these challenges? Do you notice any changes to your mood? Remember: your body and brain are closely connected!

HOW TO MAKE
a positivity poster

In need of a positivity boost? How about . . .
celebrating your achievements and best memories!
Capture things that make you feel good and the
things you've done that gave you joy.

You'll need:
- Large piece of paper
- Sticky notes
- Pens

STEP 1:

Write a piece of positivity on
each sticky note. Here are
some examples:

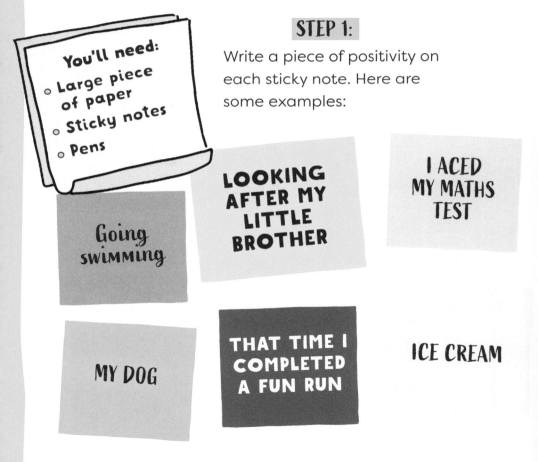

Going swimming

LOOKING AFTER MY LITTLE BROTHER

I ACED MY MATHS TEST

MY DOG

THAT TIME I COMPLETED A FUN RUN

ICE CREAM

STEP 2:

Stick your notes onto a large piece of paper to make your poster. You could decorate it too!

NOW THAT YOU HAVE YOUR POSITIVITY POSTER, YOU COULD TRY . . .

Sticking it up on the wall

When you're feeling down, take a look at your poster for some positivity power!

Creating a positivity poem

Why not turn the things you wrote on your sticky notes into a poem – it doesn't have to rhyme! Or you could try rewriting them in rhyme. Add as much detail as you like – the more you focus on the things you love, the more positivity power you will unlock!

Performing your poem

Share your poem with friends by reading it aloud – or even rapping it to a beat.

THE PENGUIN OF POETRY

DEC'S TOP TIP: Keep extra sticky notes around, so you can keep adding new achievements!

THE POWER OF SELF-CARE

Self-care means looking after yourself – and not just your body, but your mind as well. It's like saying, "Hey, I know things are busy, but right now I'm going to take the time to do something just because it makes me happy."

YOU HAVE THE POWER TO SHOW YOURSELF

LOVE and KINDNESS
by doing things you
ENJOY!

Holding my rabbit makes me really happy.

Felix, age 9

ACTIVATE YOUR POWER OF SELF-CARE

Switch on your self-care superpower in just one minute. Choose **THREE** things to do that make you feel good.

HERE ARE SOME EXAMPLES . . .

SPELL OUT YOUR NAME USING TREATS . . . THEN EAT IT!

HAVE A FIVE-MINUTE DANCE BREAK.
(See page 94–5.)

PLAY OR SING YOUR FAVOURITE SONG!

PUT ON YOUR FAVOURITE JUMPER OR YOUR FLUFFIEST SOCKS.

Remember: The things that make you feel good might be completely different from the things that make your friend feel good. Everyone is unique!

SHAKE IT OFF
A story about worries

This is a story about a snail named Sammy. Now, all snails worry about things sometimes, but Sammy worried **ALL THE TIME**.

"What if the rain washes me away?"
"What if no one wants to be friends with me?"
"What if I'm not slimy enough?"

Sammy carried his worries on his back. Every day he got slower and slower as his pile of worries grew.

Luckily, a helpful crow was passing by. "Shake off those worries," she told him. "Look, you can put them in that empty flowerpot for safekeeping."

What a great idea! Sammy's worries were safely stored and he could return to them (one at a time!) whenever he needed to – but he wasn't weighed down all the time. Phew!

HOW TO MAKE
a worry jar

You'll need:
- A large jar or container
- Paper
- Pens
- Stickers and ribbon

STEP 1:

Make sure your jar or container is clean and dry.

STEP 2:

Decorate the jar with stickers and make a paper label for the front. You could even tie a ribbon around it. Make the jar as special as you can – because your thoughts and feelings are important.

STEP 3:

The next time you feel stressed or anxious about something, write it down on a piece of paper, fold it up and put it in the worry jar. Your jar holds the worries so you don't have to!

I FEEL SO MUCH LIGHTER!

MY WORRIES

Remember: Some worries are important to share. Take a look at page 160 for more information.

WE CHALLENGE YOU

Mindfulness

So, you're packing your school bag, cleaning your teeth, watching the telly, trying to grab your book from your little sister **AND** you're panicking that you're going to be late for school. Your mind is racing and it's all starting to feel like **TOO MUCH**.

TAKE A DEEP BREATH. What is the **MOST** important thing to be doing right now? Concentrate on doing **JUST** that one thing . . . and noooooothing else.

CONGRATULATIONS!

YOU JUST PRACTISED MINDFULNESS.

Mindfulness is a big word – but it's actually pretty easy to do. It can help you feel calm and, best of all, you can do it throughout the day. Here are some small, mindful moments to get you started. Once you've tried these, why not add some of your own?

Mindful walk to school

You've probably done your walk to school a million times. But when did you last notice your surroundings? *Really* notice them? Use your senses. What colours do you see? What textures can you feel? What can you hear and smell? It's hard to worry when you're really **TUNING IN** to what's around you.

Bedtime buzzy brain

You know those nights when your head fills up with worries instead of sleep? Maybe you're worried you've upset a friend or that you won't make friends on the first day of school . . . It's OK. Take a breath, then focus on just **ONE** thought. Imagine it as a cloud floating across the sky, gently drifting away. Now focus on the next one . . . and soon you'll drift off.

Ant: Sorry, I nodded off there.

Dec: Just shows the power of mindfulness!

Remember: Thoughts are **NOT** the same as facts. See page 110–1 for more information.

ANXIETY S.O.S.

What is fear?

Everyone is frightened of something. We fear things that make us feel uncomfortable or unsafe. This is normal – it means we're human!

Ant: I'm scared of spiders. When we go to Australia for *I'm a Celebrity...Get Me Out of Here*, the spiders are **MASSIVE**. They're the size of dinner plates and there always seems to be one in my shower. I think they actually let the spiders check in to my room before I arrive!

Dec: And I'm not so keen on birds. On *I'm a Celebrity,* we ALWAYS have to do a Bushtucker Trial with birds in – I'm sure the birds know I'm scared of them! We used to do one with ostriches and I honestly thought I could hear them laughing at me when we were filming.

HA!

HA!

HA!

Human beings are wired to react when we see something scary. You probably *won't* bump into an angry sabre-toothed tiger in the loo . . . but if you did, your body would give you a burst of energy either to face your fear or run away to safety.

This is called a **'FIGHT OR FLIGHT'** response. When there **IS** real danger, feeling afraid is a very useful response.

What is anxiety?

Everyone feels anxious from time to time too. Anxiety is when you feel uneasy about something. Even though there isn't *actual* danger to run from (like that scary, toothy tiger!), your body gives you the same burst of energy. It can make your body and mind feel jumpy or restless. This isn't much fun, but it **IS** completely normal – and it **ISN'T** the same as being in danger.

The **GOOD NEWS** is that our brains are quick to adapt. With practice we can get better at understanding and managing anxious feelings.

ARGH!
THERE'S AN 'ANT'
IN MY SHOWER!

TURN OVER TO FIND SOME TIPS FOR MANAGING ANXIETY.

NEXT TIME YOU'RE FEELING ANXIOUS, HERE ARE SOME ACTIVITIES TO TRY . . .

Take a few deep breaths

Close your eyes and focus on your breath. Breathe in through your nose, and let it out slowly through your mouth.

Focus on your senses

Open your eyes. Look around and name three things you can see. Now listen. Name three sounds you can hear.

Body scan

Think about how your body is feeling. Starting from your toes and working right up to the top of your head, focus on all the different parts.

Write it down or share it

Feeling anxious is **NORMAL**. Try to put your feelings into words – write them down or tell someone you trust. Sharing often helps! If you've written your feelings down, try putting them in a worry jar (see page 121).

Positive affirmations

It's a great feeling when other people tell us reassuring things. Well, we can do the same thing for ourselves! Think of some ideas and phrases that will help you feel calm and reassured – then say them aloud to yourself or write them down.

HERE ARE A FEW IDEAS TO GET YOU STARTED . . .

I AM SAFE.

I AM IN CONTROL.

I WON'T ALWAYS FEEL LIKE THIS.

THE OCTOPUS OF CALM →

Remember: The aim isn't to get rid of anxiety for ever, but to accept how it makes you feel, in your mind and body. No feeling, including anxiety, is ever 'wrong'!

CONFIDENCE COUNTDOWN

Confidence is believing in yourself. Being confident helps you find the courage to take chances and face new challenges. No one – **ABSOLUTELY NO ONE** – feels confident all the time. Whether you're playing a sport, memorising your times tables or presenting a TV show, we all need a confidence boost sometimes.

BUILD YOUR CONFIDENCE IN . . .

5 4 3 2 1

THE SKY'S THE LIMIT!

How can you help build YOUR confidence today?

WRITE DOWN 4 THINGS THAT MAKE YOU FEEL GOOD.

MAKE EYE CONTACT WITH 3 PEOPLE.

I BELIEVE IN MYSELF!

STRIKE UP A CONVERSATION WITH 2 DIFFERENT PEOPLE.

LEARN 1 NEW THING.

What do you notice about yourself when you're feeling confident? Do you act differently? Do you speak differently? Do you react differently to challenges?

MIRROR TALK
Finding your voice

Some worries are big. Some worries are small. Big or small, your thoughts and feelings matter, and it's important to be able to share what's on your mind. If you feel worried or sad, try to find a trusted adult to talk to – it could be a parent or carer, a grandparent, a teacher or another member of staff at your school, or someone else you know well.

But sometimes – even with a trusted grown-up – it's hard to start talking. That's when it can help to practise in front of a mirror first.

I WANT TO TELL YOU ABOUT A PROBLEM I HAVE.

I'M JUST HERE TO LISTEN!

STEP 1:

Make eye contact with yourself in the mirror. Stand as tall as you can.

STEP 2:

Point to yourself in the mirror and say: "You have the right to speak out and be heard." Don't worry if it feels strange at first – that's normal. It will get lots easier, the more you practise.

STEP 3:

Tell the mirror what's bothering you. It might feel difficult. Take your time. You're in charge, and the mirror won't say anything back!

STEP 4:

Speaking out can take a lot of courage. Once you've said what's on your mind, try saying out loud that you're proud of yourself.

WELL DONE!

Remember: What you're experiencing matters. To find out how to contact Childline, turn to page 160.

NOW

IT'S TIME

to pass on the

POSITIVITY!

THE PANGOLIN
OF POSITIVITY

CHAPTER 5

PASS IT ON

So, you've celebrated what makes you unique. You've got to know your friends. You've thought about what makes you happy and challenged yourself to try some new things. Now it's time to pass on the positivity! This chapter is full of fun and creative ways to share the good vibes with others. Making other people smile feels **AMAZING**, doesn't it . . .

Be a happiness hero, and **PASS IT ON!**

WE CHALLENGE YOU

Pass the positivity parcel

Here's the great thing about spreading happiness – it's catching! When you do something that makes someone smile, they are more likely to pass it on to others, and even back to you.

THE GOOD VIBES ••• JUST KEEP GOING ROUND.

HOW CAN YOU PASS ON KINDNESS AND POSITIVITY?

Positivity parcels

It's loads of fun to wrap (and unwrap!) parcels, so why not wrap up a positive message? Write down a compliment for a friend, then challenge yourself to find a unique way of wrapping your gift – try something eco-friendly like newspaper or a recycled jar.

High-five Friday

One Friday, find five people to high-five. Then tell each of them to give five other people high-fives!

Totally awesome Tuesdays

Turn an ordinary Tuesday into a totally awesome Tuesday by choosing one person and sharing a positive message with them. Do this by saying something encouraging, or writing them a note or text message. Then ask them to pass a message on to someone. Why not challenge yourself to carry on doing it every Tuesday?

Ant: Dec, I think you look great today. I love that jacket you're wearing!

Dec: Thanks! And thanks for lending it to me!

Ant: What?

Dec: Nothing!

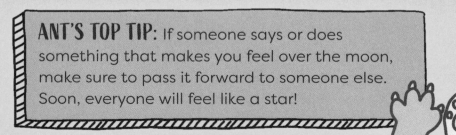

You're a star!

SO ARE YOU!

Motivation magic

Find a motivational quote in a book or on the internet, write it down (you can decorate it if you like!) and give it to a friend. Now it's their turn to find a positive quote to share with someone!

ANT'S TOP TIP: If someone says or does something that makes you feel over the moon, make sure to pass it forward to someone else. Soon, everyone will feel like a star!

POSITIVITY IS...

Giving someone a hug and telling them that I love them.

Lucas, age 9

Doing silly voices and faces! Tell a joke. Give a hug.

Lois, age 7

Saying, "You're looking nice today!"

Omar, age 9

I'll just smile and then you'll smile!

Tommy, age 9

Being kind to people and always trying to stay calm.

Seb, age 9

Pulling a funny face to make someone laugh or telling a terrible joke.

Joshua, age 10

Saying "I love you!"

Alicia, age 7

I'd do something silly like being a chicken!

Nathan, age 10

THE POWER OF SILLINESS

There's a time for being serious . . . and there's a time for being silly. Silliness can help you connect with others, as well as helping you through stressful times.

Ant: Our favourite way to be silly is to play pranks.

Dec: We do a thing on *Saturday Night Takeaway* called 'I'm a Celebrity Get Out of Me Ear', where we make celebs wear an earpiece and do whatever we tell them to. Nothing – and I mean nothing – makes us laugh more than that.

Ant: We made Anthony Joshua bark like a dog, turned Mark Wahlberg into a burger waiter and, my personal favourite, got Louis Walsh to use a banana as a mobile phone.

Dec: That was amazing! Of course, pranks are only fun if everyone is game for a laugh, so we had all of those celebrities' permission to get silly with them.

Ant: So how will **YOU** be silly? Extra points if it involves a banana . . .

ACTIVATE YOUR POWER OF SILLINESS

Ready? Steady? Time to activate your superpower of sandwiches – no, wait! – *silliness* in just one minute.

Here are **THREE** silly things you can try:

STICK A JOKER CARD TO YOUR FOREHEAD. See how long it takes for someone to mention it – and when they do, tell them a joke!

SEE HOW LONG YOU CAN BALANCE A BISCUIT ON YOUR NOSE.

EVERY TIME YOUR FRIEND ASKS YOU A QUESTION, ANSWER AS A RAP.

<u>Ant</u>: Shall we go for a jog?

<u>Dec</u>: I don't like to jog. I'd prefer to sit on a log. With my best friend ... who's a frog.

<u>Ant</u>: I thought I was your best friend.

<u>Dec</u>: You are ... I was rapping my answer.

<u>Ant</u>: Of course! Gotcha! So where did you meet him, this frog mate of yours?

<u>Dec</u>: There is no frog!

THE NOTORIOUS F.R.O.G.

PLAYTIME POWER
Let's get silly

When we see others laughing and having fun, it can instantly make us feel good. It's actual science: mirror neurons* in our brains cause us to copy behaviour and emotions that we see around us. So how do you and your friends like to have fun? Are your games noisy, calm, silly or sporty? Maybe a bit of everything?

Ant: We have a game we always play in our dressing room called Sock Football. Can you guess how it works?

Dec: If you answered, "Playing football with a rolled-up pair of socks," you win a prize! It's dead simple: one of us takes our socks off. Then we make two goals, using our bags, a chair, or whatever we can find.

Ant: Then we play Sock Football — first to score ten goals wins and the loser has to provide their socks next time — although that also means the winner has to put up with the loser's smelly feet!

Dec: Just one tip — no headers. After all, who wants to put their head on someone else's smelly socks!

* Tiny cells in our brains that become active when we watch others.

HOW WILL YOU SHARE THE FUN?

HERE ARE SOME FUN ACTIVITIES TO SHARE WITH YOUR FRIENDS – AND PASS ON THAT POSITIVITY!

The circle of stares

Everyone stands in a circle. Choose one person to call "Look down" or "Look up". When it's "Look down", look at the ground. When it's "Look up", look at someone else in the circle. If they're staring right back at you, you're both out – so go out as dramatically as you can! Keep playing until there are just two people left – they're the winners.

OH, I DIDN'T SEE YOU THERE!

Human rock, paper, scissors

You've probably played this game before, but have you used your whole body – not just your hands? Crouch into a ball if you're a rock. Lie flat on the ground if you're paper. And if you're scissors, stand tall with your legs and arms apart, then bring your hands together above your head like scissors.

TURN OVER FOR MORE SUPER SILLY GAMES!

Friend-a-thon

Ask each person to choose an event. Now split into two teams – the winning team is the first to complete ALL the events! For example, you and your friends might choose running, building a tower of playing cards, going across the monkey bars and making a jam sandwich. Congratulations! You've just invented the run-build-monkey-jam-a-thon!

Body-spell buddies

Gather as many friends as you can for this body-spell challenge! Can you use your bodies to make the letters of the word: 'FRIENDSHIP'? How about 'GOAT'? Choose your own favourite words or names, and ask someone to take a photograph!

Musical mates

Pick your favourite song. Now take turns singing it – one word at a time! If you miss a word, go back to the start. If you can make it all the way through, you're musical stars!

Sundae fun-day

Host an ice-cream party and ask each friend to bring a different topping. (Don't forget to check if any of your guests have an allergy or intolerance.) Will they bring chocolate buttons? Gummy bears? Hundreds and thousands? Banana slices? The list is endless – and delicious! Now everyone gets to decorate their ice-cream sundaes with whichever toppings they like. Try making up special names for your tasty creations too!

Why not invent your own games?

THE ONLY LIMIT IS ● ● ●
YOUR IMAGINATION!

My brother and I play this game where we pretend to audition for *Britain's Got Talent*. My brother, who is four, once said, "Hello my name is Kabir . . . and I come from Sainsbury's." We couldn't stop laughing!

Dhiya, age 9

WE CHALLENGE YOU

Laugh it up!

Laughter is good for you. You may have heard that exercise boosts health and releases endorphins (chemicals that give us a happy feeling), but did you know that laughing does that too? Laughter also brings people together. You are 30 times more likely to laugh in a group than alone. (Try it with the jokes on pages 62–3 and 90–1!)

Ant: I can't think of anyone in the world I'd rather have a laugh with than you, Dec.

Dec: Thanks! I can't think of anyone else I'd rather share a joke with than you, Ant.

Ant: Thanks!

Dec: Except maybe Stephen Mulhern. He's **SO** funny!

Ant: What?

Dec: Or there's my postman, now he's a REALLY funny guy ...

THE LOBSTER OF LAUGHTER

FOR A LAUGH, TRY THESE GIGGLESOME CHALLENGES . . .

Funny movie bingo

Choose a funny movie to watch. Before you start, create bingo cards with words or actions that make you laugh. For example: 'Someone farts'. If someone does it in the movie, race to be the first one to tick it off your card!

Joke collector

Write down or record all the jokes you hear in a week. Which ones make you laugh the most?

What's the difference between a unicorn and a field of carrots?

ONE'S A FUNNY BEAST, THE OTHER'S A BUNNY FEAST!

Pot-luck jokes

Write some jokes on pieces of paper and put them in a bag or hat. Ask people to take a joke from the bag and tell it to you in the silliest way they can.

Remember: Sometimes you might not feel like laughing and that's OK too.

MONSTER MASH-UP
Share your creativity

Ant: We love working together on new projects and ideas. Collaborating with a friend helps you come up with better, more interesting ideas. Why? Because everyone is different and will bring their own unique perspective!

Dec: Remember, there's no such thing as a bad idea...

Ant: Apart from your idea for chocolate toothpaste!

Dec: Working together is why we love the game Monster Mash-up. The more players you have, the sillier your monster will be!

You'll need:

○ Paper
○ Coloured pens
○ A friend or several!

HOW TO PLAY:

STEP 1:

Fold a piece of paper widthways, then fold it again. You should have four thin sections.

STEP 2:

Draw your monster's head in the top section – don't let anyone see! Now fold it over to hide it.

146

STEP 3:

Give your paper to the next person so they can draw the body. They then fold the paper to hide their drawing.

STEP 4:

Pass to the next person so they can draw the legs. Fold the paper and pass it on.

STEP 5:

The final person draws the feet, shoes or smelly socks! Now unfold your drawing to see what your monster looks like!

ANT & DEC'S MONSTER:

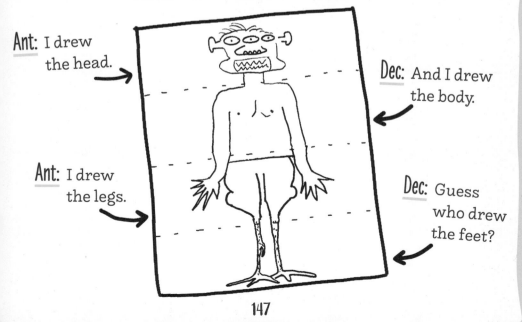

Ant: I drew the head.

Dec: And I drew the body.

Ant: I drew the legs.

Dec: Guess who drew the feet?

WE CHALLENGE YOU

Theme day

Who says you need an excuse to plan a day of fun? A theme day, with games and snacks – and maybe even costumes! – is an amazing way to pass on the positivity.

WHAT'S YOUR PERFECT THEME?
HERE ARE SOME IDEAS . . .

Backwards day

Turn those T-shirts back to front and wear sunglasses on the back of your head. Eat your dinner for breakfast, and breakfast for dinner. Do you have a favourite book? Start reading it backwards! Remember, your names must be backwards too . . .

Ant: Hi, Ced!

Dec: Hi, Tna!

I THOUGHT YOU SAID UPSIDE DOWN?

ANT'S TOP TIP: It doesn't matter what your theme is. What matters is that you're together and having a blast! Check with your parent or guardian to make sure they're OK with your theme and activities.

Pirate day

Today, everyone must speak like
a pirate, or else ye will walk the
plank! Make a treasure hunt for
everyone, with gold (chocolate!)
coins as the prize!

Ant: And if anyone asks "Why are you
dressed like pirates?", you **HAVE**
to reply, "Because we aaaaarrrrrrr!"

Christmas day

It doesn't matter if it's the middle of July, you can
still have a Christmas-themed day! Make paper
snowflakes. Wear your favourite festive jumper.
Sing Christmas songs and play festive games like
'Pin the Beard on Santa'. **HO, HO, HO!**

Yes day

The only rule is: you and your friends have to say
yes to everything each one of you suggests!
(Unless it's dangerous, illegal or makes you
feel uncomfortable.) Will you end up wearing
fake moustaches while you go to the shop?
The answer might be . . . **YES**!

CHANGE-MAKERS

Another amazing way to pass on the positivity is by making change. Whether it's helping our friends and family or the environment, we can all do our bit to create a better world. Even the small actions of one person can make a big difference!

WANT TO BE A CHANGE-MAKER? HERE ARE SOME SIMPLE THINGS YOU COULD DO TO HELP . . .

Sustainable swapping

Instead of buying new clothing, books or games, you could set up a swap with your friends! (Be sure to ask a parent or guardian first.) Bring what you don't wear or use any more, and swap it for stuff that feels like new! (Remember: you don't HAVE to swap – there are always going to be things you will want to keep!)

ANYONE WANT TO SWAP SHELLS?

Switch off!

You can save energy by switching off lights when you don't need them. For another challenge, try a screen-free day: try to go 24 hours without turning on the TV, a mobile phone or tablet!

Sharing and caring

Do you have any books or toys that you don't use any more? You could donate them to a local shelter or a children's hospital. You could even organise a food drive in your neighbourhood or at school to collect food for donating to a food bank.

Clean up!

Challenge your friends to go litter-picking with you. Get permission from your adult first! Wear thick, old gloves or get hold of a litter-picker – and be careful not to touch anything broken or sharp. You could even make it into a game: whoever picks the most litter wins!

Remember:

EVEN **BIG** CHANGES START WITH

SMALL STEPS!

WE CHALLENGE YOU

Karaoke spectacular

Singing in the shower! Singing in front of the mirror! Singing alone or together! Not only does it help with stress, but it's also a great way to express yourself. Try this super silly challenge and share the fun!

Ant: And if you haven't got a perfect singing voice, we've got news for you …

Dec: That makes it even **MORE** fun!

A MILLION PER CENT YES!